Geometry and Measurement Grade 4 Math Essentials

Children's Geometry Books

Speedy Publishing LLC
40 E. Main St. #1156
Newark, DE 19711
www.speedypublishing.com

Exercise Number: 1

Name: ______________________________ Score: ____

Converting Measurements

1. 3 C = ______ oz

2. 2 yd = ______ ft

3. 132 in = ______ ft

4. 2 qt = ______ pt

5. 7 yd = ______ ft

6. 8 lb = ______ oz

Exercise Number: 2

Name: ______________________ Score: ____

Converting Measurements

1. 5 lb = ________ oz

2. 2 C = ______ pt

3. 1 qt = ______ C

4. 4 lb = ________ oz

5. 5 gal = ______ qt

6. 6 gal = ______ qt

Exercise Number: 3

Name:______________________________ Score:____

Converting Measurements

1. 10 C = _____ pt

4. 8 C = _____ qt

2. 12 C = _____ qt

5. 3 gal = _____ qt

3. 15 ft = _____ yd

6. 4 qt = _____ pt

Exercise Number: 4

Name: ______________________________ Score: ____

Converting Measurements

1. 7 gal = _____ qt

4. 24 qt = ____ gal

2. 64 oz = _____ C

5. 60 in = _____ ft

3. 4 qt = _____ C

6. 3 qt = _____ C

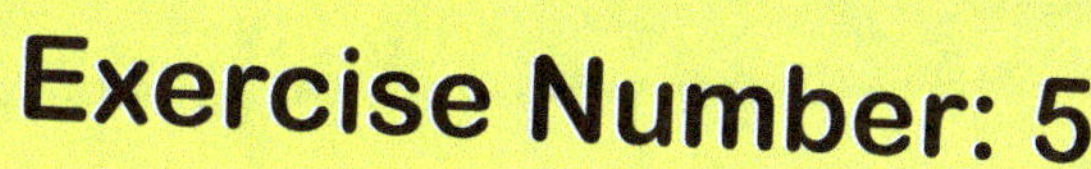

Exercise Number: 5

Name: ______________________________ Score: ____

Converting Measurements

1. 6 C = _____ pt

4. 20 qt = ____ gal

2. 1 C = ______ oz

5. 3 gal = ______ qt

3. 7 pt = _____ C

6. 6 ft = _____ yd

Exercise Number: 6

Name: ______________________________ Score: ____

Converting Measurements

1. 4 qt = ____ gal

2. 1 qt = ______ pt

3. 2 qt = ______ C

4. 40 oz = _____ C

5. 1 lb = ________ oz

6. 16 qt = ____ gal

Exercise Number: 7

Name: ______________________________ Score: ____

Converting Measurements

1. 4 pt = _____ C

4. 16 C = _____ pt

2. 2 qt = _____ pt

5. 132 in = _____ ft

3. 5 yd = _____ ft

6. 2 qt = _____ pt

Exercise Number: 8

Name: ______________________________ Score: ____

Converting Measurements

1. 8 pt = _____ qt

2. 16 oz = _____ C

3. 5 pt = _____ C

4. 3 ft = _____ yd

5. 8 C = _____ qt

6. 27 ft = _____ yd

Exercise Number: 9

Name:______________________________ Score:____

Converting Measurements

1. 32 oz = _____ lb
2. 6 ft = _____ yd
3. 11 yd = _____ ft
4. 12 C = _____ pt
5. 7 lb = _______ oz
6. 4 C = _____ qt

Exercise Number: 10

Name: ______________________________ Score: ____

Converting Measurements

1. 12 C = _____ qt

4. 16 qt = _____ gal

2. 5 C = _____ oz

5. 1 pt = _____ C

3. 2 gal = _____ qt

6. 120 in = _____ ft

Exercise Number: 11

Name:______________________________ Score:____

Converting Measurements

1. 4 C = _____ qt

4. 2 lb = _______ oz

2. 6 yd = ______ ft

5. 48 oz = _____ lb

3. 12 ft = _____ yd

6. 27 ft = _____ yd

Exercise Number: 12

Name: ______________________________ Score: ____

Converting Measurements

1. 3 ft = ________ in

4. 2 pt = ______ qt

2. 12 ft = ________ in

5. 3 qt = _______ C

3. 7 yd = ______ ft

6. 56 oz = ______ C

Exercise Number: 13

Name:______________________________ Score:____

Converting Measurements

1. 5 pt = _____ C

2. 10 ft = _______ in

3. 4 lb = ________ oz

4. 48 oz = _____ C

5. 7 ft = _______ in

6. 3 gal = ______ qt

Exercise Number: 14

Name: ______________________________ Score: ____

Converting Measurements

1. 4 pt = _____ qt

4. 2 qt = ______ pt

2. 10 lb = ________ oz

5. 5 ft = ________ in

3. 3 qt = ______ pt

6. 3 yd = ______ ft

Exercise Number: 15

Name:______________________________ Score:____

Converting Measurements

1. 84 in = ______ ft

4. 3 lb = ________ oz

2. 144 oz = _____ lb

5. 7 pt = _____ C

3. 8 qt = ____ gal

6. 32 oz = _____ lb

Exercise Number: 16

Name: ____________________ Score: ____

Converting Measurements

1. 128 oz = _____ lb

2. 16 C = _____ qt

3. 6 C = _____ pt

4. 48 oz = _____ C

5. 3 qt = _____ C

6. 72 in = _____ ft

Exercise Number: 17

Name: ______________________________ Score: ____

Converting Measurements

1. 4 qt = ______ pt

4. 6 pt = _____ C

2. 16 qt = ____ gal

5. 7 C = ______ oz

3. 12 yd = ______ ft

6. 16 C = _____ pt

Exercise Number: 18

Name: ______________________________ Score: ____

Converting Measurements

1. 12 C = _____ qt

2. 8 lb = ________ oz

3. 6 ft = _____ yd

4. 1 lb = ________ oz

5. 16 C = _____ qt

6. 6 lb = ________ oz

Exercise Number: 19

Name: ______________________ Score: ____

Solve.

6

6

Area = ____

Perimeter = ____

Exercise Number: 20

Name: ______________________________ Score: ____

Solve.

8

8

Area = ____

Perimeter = ____

Exercise Number: 21

Name: ______________________________ Score: ____

Solve.

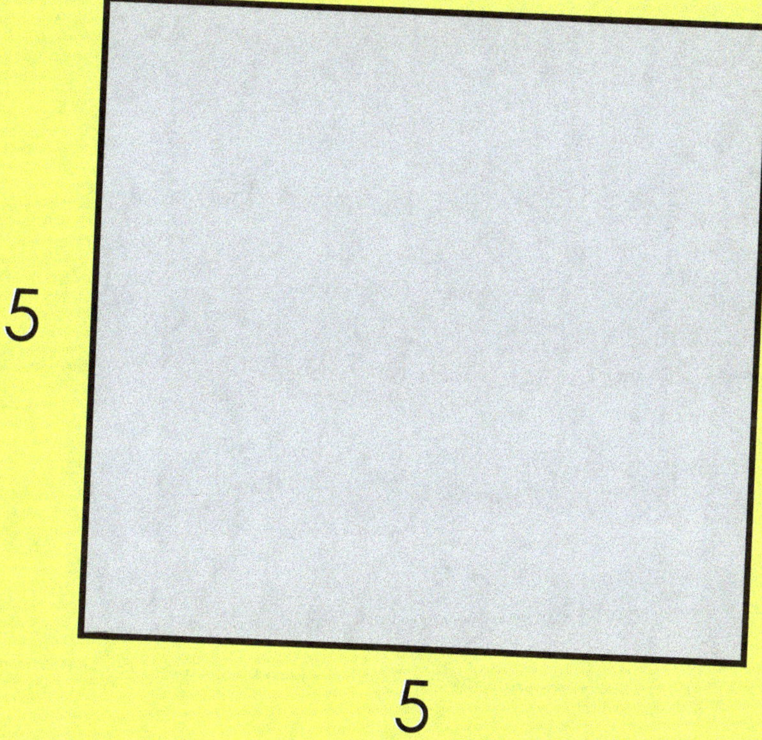

Area = ____

Perimeter = ____

Exercise Number: 22

Name: ______________________ Score: ____

Solve.

4

4

Area = ____

Perimeter = ____

Exercise Number: 23

Name: ________________________ Score: ____

Solve.

8

5

Area = ____

Perimeter = ____

Exercise Number: 24

Name: ______________________ Score: ____

Solve.

Area = ____

Perimeter = ____

Exercise Number: 25

Name: ______________________________ Score: ____

Solve.

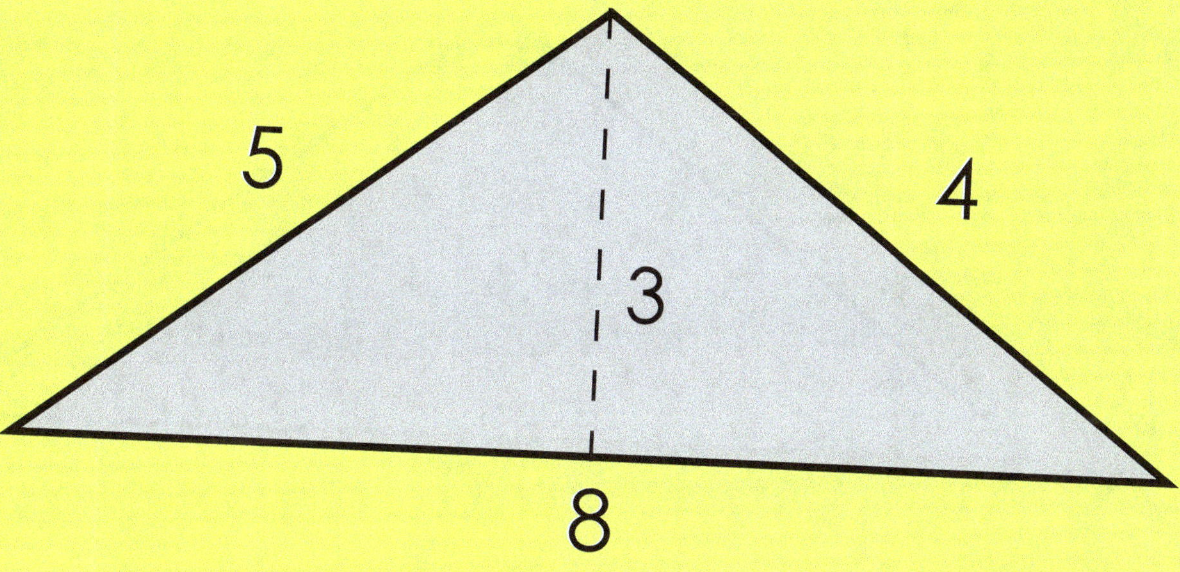

Area = ____

Perimeter = ____

Exercise Number: 26

Name: ______________________________ Score: ____

Solve.

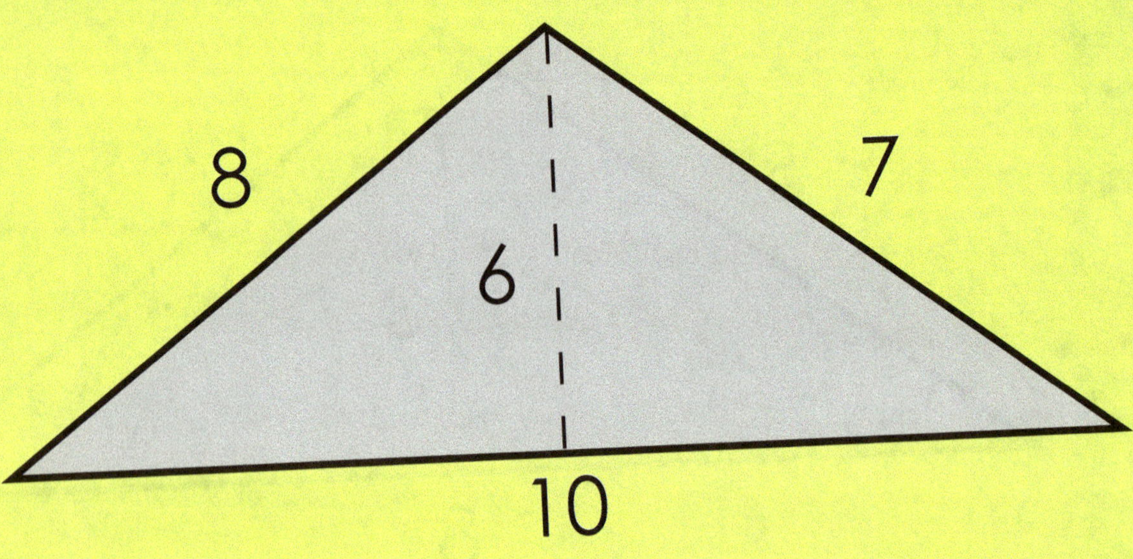

Area = ____

Perimeter = ____

Exercise Number: 27

Name: ______________________ Score: ____

Solve.

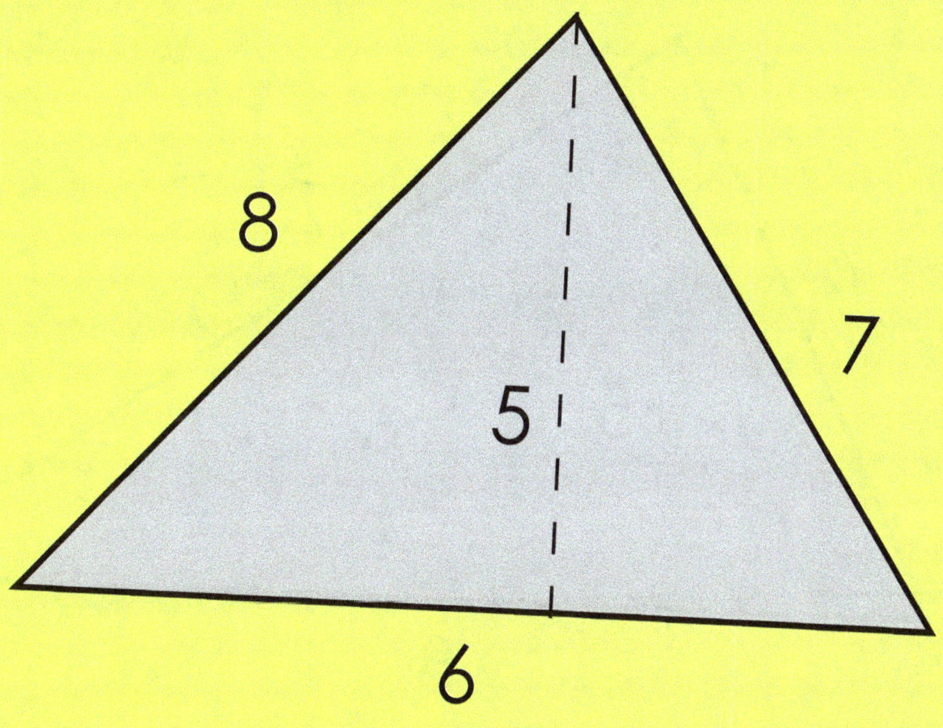

Area = ____

Perimeter = ____

Exercise Number: 28

Name: ______________________________ Score: ____

Solve.

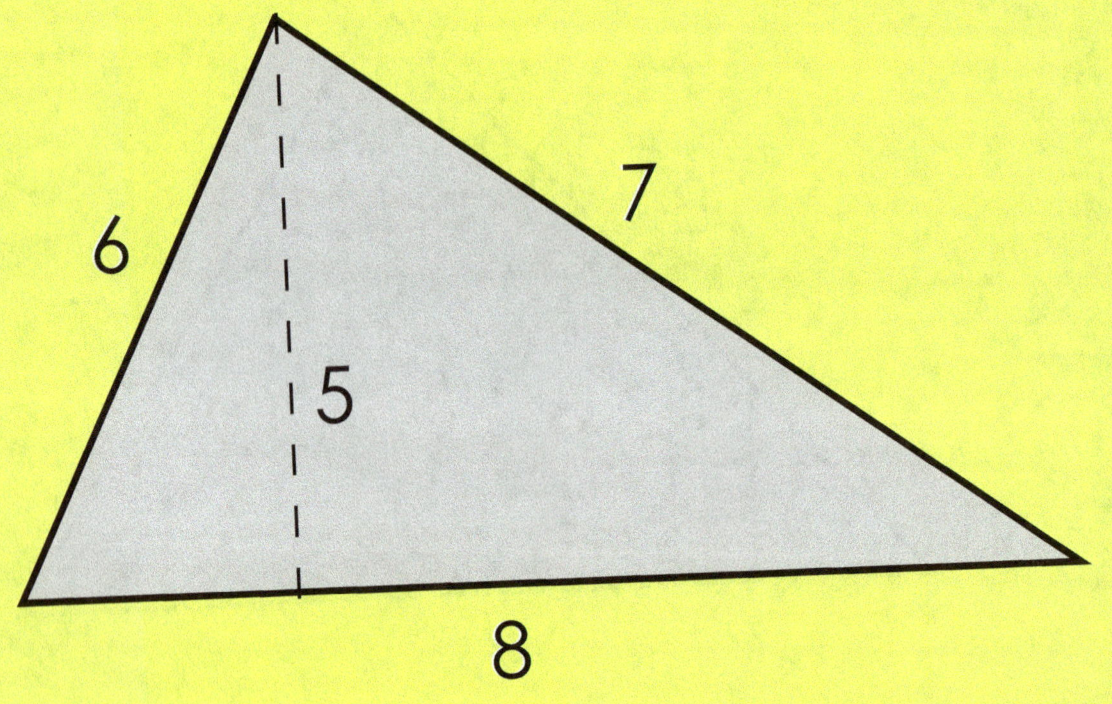

Area = ____

Perimeter = ____

Exercise Number: 29

Name: ______________________________ Score: ____

Solve.

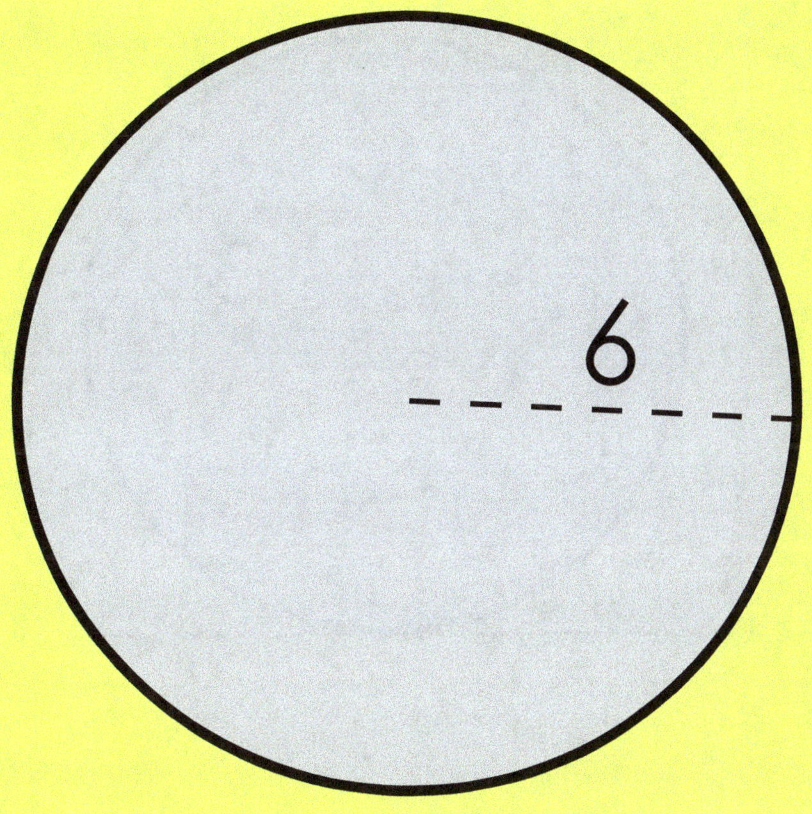

Circumference = ____

Diameter = ____

Exercise Number: 30

Name: ______________________________ Score: ____

Solve.

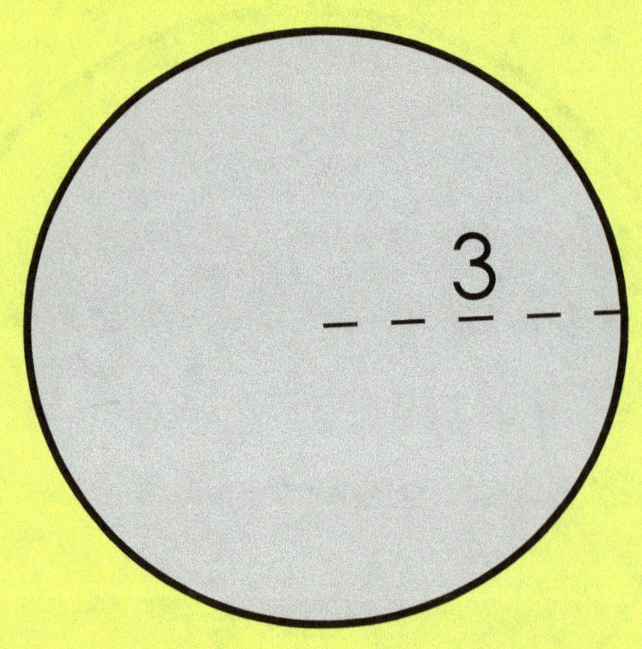

Circumference = ____

Diameter = ____

Exercise Number: 31

Name: ______________________ Score: ____

Solve.

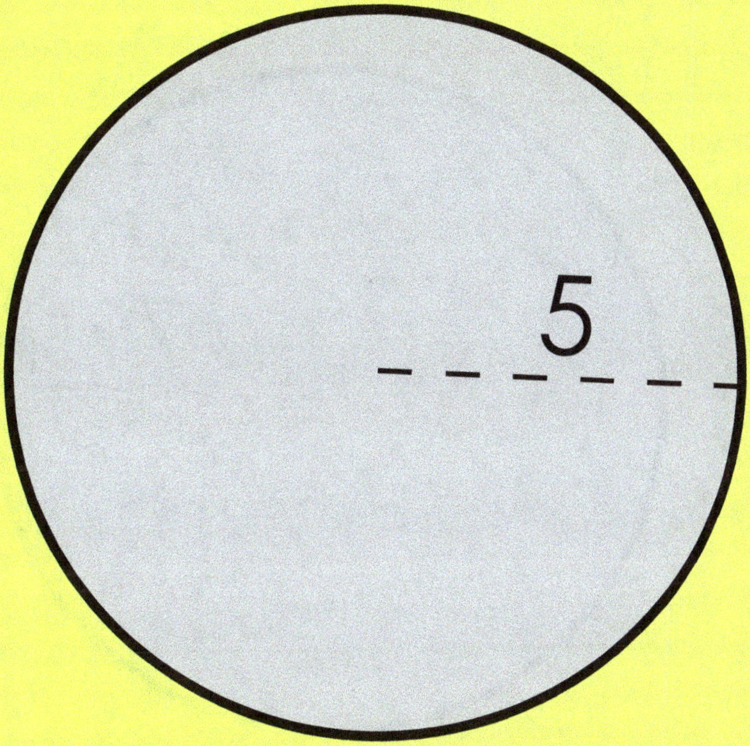

5

Circumference = ____

Diameter = ____

Exercise Number: 32

Name: ______________________ Score: ____

Solve.

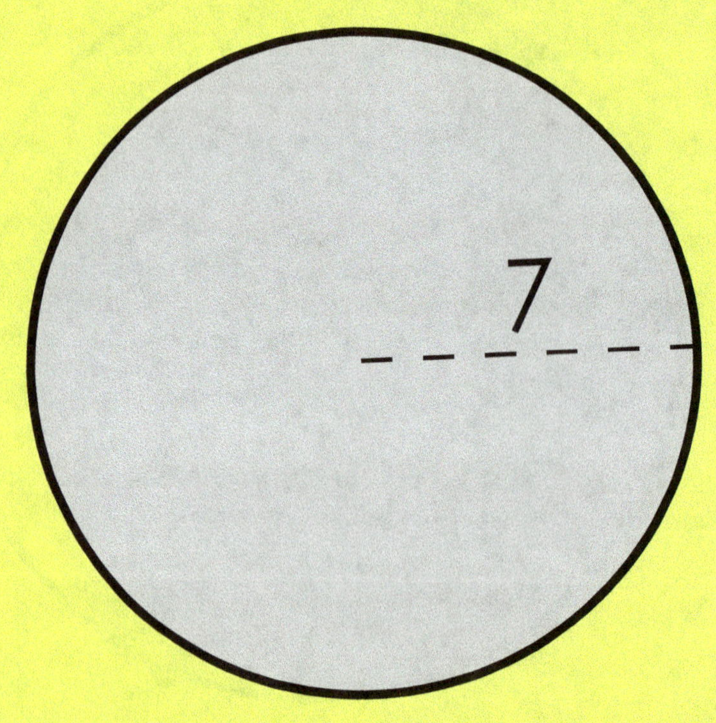

Circumference = ____

Diameter = ____

Exercise Number: 33

Name: ______________________ Score: ____

Solve.

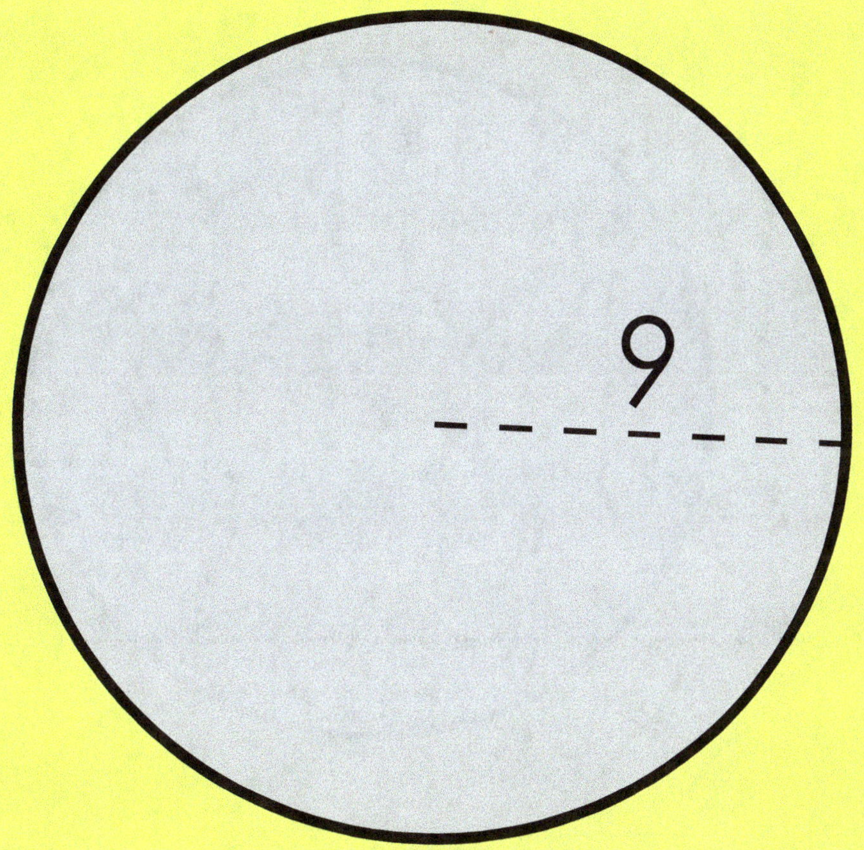

Circumference = ____

Diameter = ____

Exercise Number: 34

Name: ______________________ Score: ____

Solve.

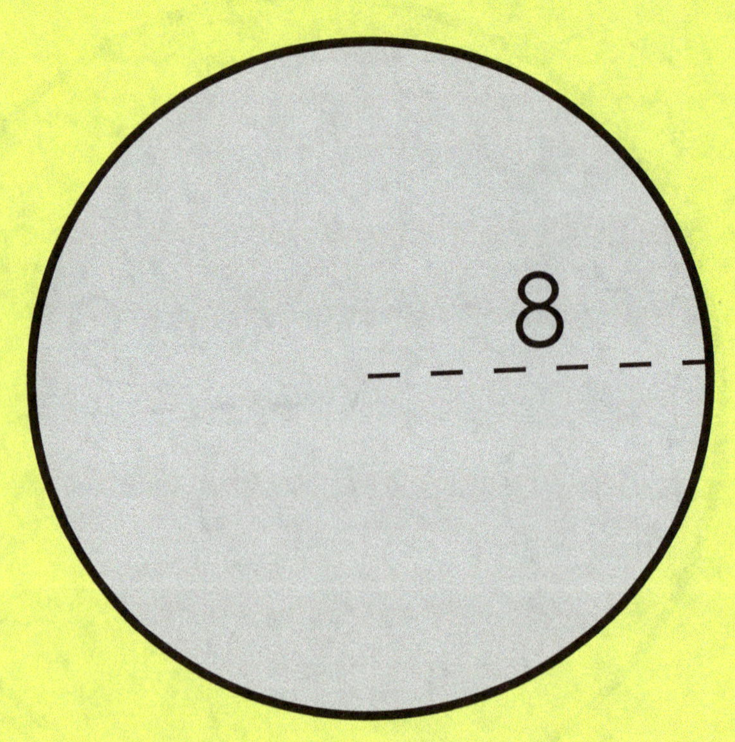

Circumference = ____

Diameter = ____

Exercise Number: 35

Name: ______________________ Score: ____

Solve.

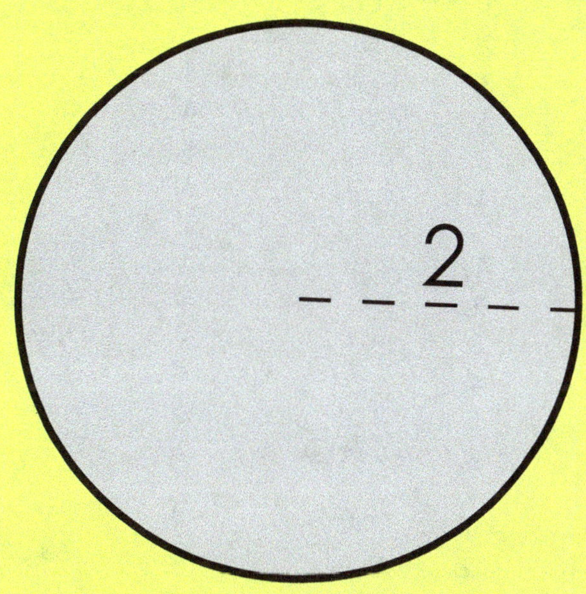

Circumference = ____

Diameter = ____

ANSWERS

1. 24 oz
2. 6 ft
3. 11 ft
4. 4 pt
5. 21 ft
6. 128 oz

1. 80 oz
2. 1 pt
3. 4 C
4. 64 oz
5. 20 qt
6. 24 qt

1. 5 pt
2. 3 qt
3. 5 yd
4. 2 qt
5. 12 qt
6. 8 pt

1. 28 qt
2. 8 C
3. 16 C
4. 6 gal
5. 5 ft
6. 12 C

1. 3 pt
2. 8 oz
3. 14 C
4. 5 gal
5. 12 qt
6. 2 yd

1. 1 gal
2. 2 pt
3. 8 C
4. 5 C
5. 16 oz
6. 4 gal

1. 8 C
2. 4 pt
3. 15 ft
4. 8 pt
5. 11 ft
6. 4 pt

1. 4 qt
2. 2 C
3. 10 C
4. 1 yd
5. 2 qt
6. 9 yd

1. 2 lb
2. 2 yd
3. 33 ft
4. 6 pt
5. 112 oz
6. 1 qt

1. 3 qt
2. 40 oz
3. 8 qt
4. 4 gal
5. 2 C
6. 10 ft

1. 1 qt
2. 18 ft
3. 4 yd
4. 32 oz
5. 3 lb
6. 9 yd

1. 36 in
2. 144 in
3. 21 ft
4. 1 qt
5. 12 C
6. 7 C

1. 10 C
2. 120 in
3. 64 oz
4. 6 C
5. 84 in
6. 12 qt

1. 2 qt
2. 160 oz
3. 6 pt
4. 4 pt
5. 60 in
6. 9 ft

1. 7 ft
2. 9 lb
3. 2 gal
4. 48 oz
5. 14 C
6. 2 lb

1. 8 lb
2. 4 qt
3. 3 pt
4. 6 C
5. 12 C
6. 6 ft

1. 8 pt
2. 4 gal
3. 36 ft
4. 12 C
5. 56 oz
6. 8 pt

1. 3 qt
2. 128 oz
3. 2 yd
4. 16 oz
5. 4 qt
6. 96 oz

ANSWERS

Area = 36
Perimeter = 24

Area = 64
Perimeter = 32

Area = 25
Perimeter = 20

Area = 16
Perimeter = 16

Area = 26
Perimeter = 40

Area = 22
Perimeter = 24

Area = 17
Perimeter = 12

Area = 25
Perimeter = 30

Area = 21
Perimeter = 15

Area = 21
Perimeter = 20

Circumference = 37.7
Diameter = 12

Circumference = 18.85
Diameter = 6

Circumference = 31.42
Diameter = 10

Circumference = 43.98
Diameter = 14

Circumference = 56.55
Diameter = 18

Circumference = 50.27
Diameter = 16

Circumference = 12.57
Diameter = 4

www.ingramcontent.com/pod-product-compliance
Lightning Source LLC
LaVergne TN
LVHW082307150826
845677LV00009B/1738